F-16 FIGHTING FALCONS

BY JACK DAVID

BELLWETHER MEDIA · MINNEAPOLIS, MN

Are you ready to take it to the extreme?
Torque books thrust you into the action-packed
world of sports, vehicles, and adventure. These books
may include dirt, smoke, fire, and dangerous stunts.
WARNING: read at your own risk.

Library of Congress Cataloging-in-Publication Data

Library of Congress Cataloging-in-Publication Data

David, Jack, 1968-
  F-16 Fighting Falcons / by Jack David.
     p. cm. -- (Torque, military machines)
  Summary: "Explains the technologies and capabilities of the latest generation of F-16 planes.
Intended for grades 3 through 7 "--Provided by publisher.
  Includes bibliographical references and index.
  ISBN-13: 978-1-60014-104-1 (hbk : alk. paper)
  ISBN-10: 1-60014-104-8 (hbk : alk. paper)
  1. F-16 (Jet fighter plane)--Juvenile literature. I. Title. II. Series.

  UG1242.F5D3467 2008
  623.74'64--dc22

                                                                        2007012161

This edition first published in 2008 by Bellwether Media.

The photographs in this book are reproduced through the courtesy of the United States Department of
Defense.

CONTENTS

THE F-16 IN ACTION 4

MULTI-ROLE FIGHTER 10

WEAPONS 14

F-16 MISSIONS 18

GLOSSARY 22

TO LEARN MORE 23

INDEX 24

THE F-16 IN ACTION

Four F-16 Fighting Falcons speed toward a group of enemy planes. The enemy planes are flying toward a U.S. Air Force base. The F-16s race through the sky shooting flames from their jet engines. They have the enemy planes in weapons range in minutes.

★ **FAST FACT** ★

Since 1974, over 4,000 F-16s have been built worldwide.

The F-16 pilots fire their **missiles**. An explosion fills the sky. One of the enemy planes is destroyed.

The rest of the enemy planes turn around. They know their planes cannot match the speed and firepower of the F-16s. The U.S. base is safe. The F-16s have completed their **mission** and turn toward home.

MULTI-ROLE FIGHTER

The F-16 Fighting Falcon is one of the Air Force's best fighter planes. The Air Force has used it for a variety of missions since 1979. F-16s can fight enemy planes or serve as bombers. They can also protect other aircraft such as cargo planes.

★ **FAST FACT** ★

The F-16 has a top speed of 1,500 mph (2414 km/h).

F-16 SPECIFICATIONS:

Primary Function: Multi-role fighter

Length: 49 feet (15 meters)

Height: 16 feet (5 meters)

Wingspan: 32 feet (10 meters)

Speed: 1,500 mph (2,414 km/h)

Range: 2000 miles (3,219 kilometers)

Ceiling: 50,000 feet (15,240 meters)

Weight: 37,500 pounds (17,000 kilograms)

The crew loads the missiles.

A crew member checks the missile system.

The F-16's great speed is important to these roles. The F-16 has powerful jet engines. The engines can push the F-16 to more than 1,500 miles (2,414 kilometers) per hour. That's about twice the speed of sound. This is why the F-16 is called a **supersonic** fighter plane.

13

WEAPONS

F-16 pilots use powerful weapons to destroy targets. The F-16's most basic weapon is its M61 **machine gun**. This gun can shoot 100 rounds per second.

The F-16 canopy provides a good view f...

★ FAST FAC

The F-16's "bubble" canopy makes it ideal for air-to... combat, or "dog fights."

Another important F-16 weapon is the Sidewinder missile. The Sidewinder is an air-to-air missile. This means that F-16 pilots fire Sidewinders at other planes in the air.

F-16s also carry air-to-ground (AGM) weapons. Pilots can launch **laser-guided bombs** and AGM-88 guided missiles against ground targets. F-16s can even carry nuclear missiles.

F-16 MISSIONS

F-16 pilots perform most missions in groups. Pilots protect each other by flying in **formation**. Pilots discuss plans with each other over radios. They work together to carry out their orders.

★ **FAST FACT** ★

A F-16's engine can produce 27,000 lbs (12,247 kg) of thrust.

F-16s have been an important part of the U.S. Air Force for a long time. They have flown thousands of missions. The plane's high speed, powerful weapons, and skilled pilots have kept them useful and valuable. They remain one of the most effective fighter planes in the world.

GLOSSARY

formation—the pattern in which a group of planes fly

laser-guided bomb—an explosive that locks onto a target after troops mark it with a laser beam

machine gun—an automatic weapon that fires bullets rapidly

missile—an explosive launched at targets on the ground or in the air

mission—a military task

supersonic—able to move faster than the speed of sound

TO LEARN MORE

AT THE LIBRARY
Braulick, Carrie A. *U.S. Air Force Fighters*. Mankato, Minn.: Capstone Press, 2007.

Cooper, Jason. *U.S. Air Force*. Vero Beach, Fla.: Rourke, 2004.

Doeden, Matt. *The U.S. Air Force*. Mankato, Minn.: Capstone Press, 2005.

ON THE WEB
Learning more about military machines
is as easy as 1, 2, 3.

1. Go to www.factsurfer.com

2. Enter "military machines" into search box.

3. Click the "Surf" button and you will see a list of related web sites.

With factsurfer.com, finding more information is just a click away.

INDEX

AGM-88 guided missiles, 17

air-to-air missile, 17

air-to-ground weapons, 17

bombers, 10

cargo planes, 10

enemy planes, 4, 7, 9, 10

fighter plane, 10, 13, 21

firepower, 9

formations, 18

jet engines, 4, 13, 18

laser-guided bombs, 17

M61 machine gun, 14

missiles, 7, 16, 17

missions, 9, 10, 18, 21

nuclear missiles, 17

pilots, 7, 14, 15, 17, 18, 21

radios, 18

Sidewinder missile, 17

speed of sound, 13

supersonic fighter plane, 13

targets, 14, 17

U.S. Air Force, 10, 21

U.S. Air Force base, 4

weapons, 4, 7, 14, 16, 17, 21